PowerKids Readers:

ROAD MACHINES™

Road Rollers

Joanne Randolph

The Rosen Publishing Group's
PowerKids Press™
New York

For Joseph Hobson, with love

PM JV

Published in 2002 by The Rosen Publishing Group, Inc.
29 East 21st Street, New York, NY 10010

Copyright © 2002 by The Rosen Publishing Group, Inc.

First Edition

Book Design: Michael Donnellan

Photo Credits: All photos by Antonio Mari

Randolph, Joanne.
Road rollers / Joanne Randolph.
    p. cm. — (Road machines)
Includes bibliographical references and index.
  ISBN 0–8239–6037–4 (library binding)
1. Road rollers—Juvenile literature. [1. Road rollers.] I. Title.
  TE223 .R36 2002
  625.8'5—dc21

                                            2001000134

Manufactured in the United States of America

Contents

A road roller is a
road machine.

Road rollers work
on our roads.

7

This road roller flattens
new tar. Tar is what makes
up a road.

A road roller's job is to smooth out the bumps. It spreads and flattens.

A road roller has big metal wheels. The wheels are shaped like big round cans.

13

The big metal wheels
help the road roller to do
its job.

15

A person drives the road roller. The driver steers it in straight lines.

17

A road roller must drive back and forth. The driver must make sure the tar is smooth.

19

Road rollers do good
work for our roads.

21

Words to Know

wheel

road roller

tar

Here are more books to read about road rollers:

Building a Road
(Machines at Work)
by Arthur Pluckrose
Franklin Watts, Inc.

Diggers and Other Construction Machines
by Jon Richards
Copper Beach Books

To learn more about road rollers, check out this Web site:
www.field-guides.com/html/compactors.html

Index

Word Count: 105

Note to Librarians, Teachers, and Parents

PowerKids Readers are specially designed to help emergent and beginning readers build their skills in reading for information. Simple vocabulary and concepts are paired with photographs of real kids in real-life situations or stunning, detailed images from the world around them. Readers will respond to written language by linking meaning with their own everyday experiences and observations. Sentences are short and simple, employing a basic vocabulary of sight words, as well as new words that describe objects or processes that take place in the world. Large type, clean design, and photographs corresponding directly to the text all help children to decipher meaning. Features such as a contents page, picture glossary, and index help children get the most out of PowerKids Readers. They also introduce children to the basic elements of a book, which they will encounter in their future reading experiences. Lists of related books and Web sites encourage kids to explore other sources and to continue the process of learning.